BOXCAR MOLLY

A Story From the Great Depression

SURVIVORS

BOXCAR MOLLY

A Story From the Great Depression

James Riordan

HODDER
Wayland

an imprint of Hodder Children's Books

Acknowledgements:

Brother, Can You Spare a Dime? Words by E. Y. Harburg,
music by Jay Gorney, 1932, Harms Inc.
Used by permission of Warner Bros – Seven Artists Music

John Steinbeck, *The Grapes of Wrath* (Heinemann, London, 1939)

Text copyright © 2002 James Riordan
Volume copyright © 2002 Hodder Wayland

Book editor: Katie Orchard
Map illustrator: Peter Bull

Published in Great Britain in 2002 by Hodder Wayland
An imprint of Hodder Children's Books Limited

The right of James Riordan to be identified as the author of
this Work has been asserted by him in accordance with
the Copyright, Designs and Patents Act 1988.

British Library Cataloguing in Publication Data

Riordan, James 1936–
Boxcar Molly: A Story From the Great Depression. – (Survivors)
1. Depressions – 1929 2. Children's stories
I. Title
823.9'14 [J]

ISBN 0 7502 3786 4

Typeset by Avon Dataset Ltd, Bidford-on-Avon, Warks
www.avondataset.com

Printed and bound in Great Britain by
Clays Ltd, St Ives plc

Introduction

On 'Black Thursday', the last day of October 1929, American newspapers screamed:

MARKET CRASH – PANIC HITS NATION!

How could it happen? The United States of America was the richest nation in the world. American business was as solid as the Rock of Gibraltar. Yet, suddenly, the bubble burst and everyone began to sell their stocks and shares. In just a few days, prices on the Wall Street Stock Exchange crashed.

Wall Street was like a zoo where all the animals had gone crazy, roaring and fighting each other. Men rushed out into the street, yelling, 'I'm bust!' and, 'I'm sold out!' Some even killed themselves, like the 'Match King', Ivan Kreuger. Most of the nation's savings went down the drain. Over 5,000 banks closed. Factories laid off millions of workers. The army of jobless people grew from 1.5 million in 1929 to 13 million in 1932 – a third of the work-force.

Millions of Americans were now stripped of everything:

jobs, homes, possessions, food. Some slept on rubbish dumps to keep warm, scrabbling over them for food, competing with the flies and maggots.

Some towns set up 'soup-kitchens' to feed the starving. At the same time, stores had millions of tonnes of food – but it wasn't profitable to sell at prices that might double the next day. Warehouses were full of clothes – yet people couldn't afford to buy them. Houses were plentiful – but they stayed empty because people couldn't pay the rent. So families lived in shacks in shanty towns called 'Hoovervilles', named after Herbert Hoover, the US President at the time, and they slept under newspapers, which became known as 'Hoover blankets'.

This is the story of ordinary Americans in the Great Depression. Although the central characters in the story are fictional, as far as possible the story describes real events and retains real names.

And a homeless hungry man, driving the road with his wife beside him and his thin children in the back seat, could look at the fallow fields which might produce food but not profit, and that man could know how a fallow field is a sin and the unused land a crime against the thin children . . .

And in the south he saw the golden oranges hanging on the trees, the little golden oranges on the dark green trees; and guards with shotguns patrolling the lines so a man might not pick an orange for a thin child, oranges to be dumped if the price was low.

(John Steinbeck, *The Grapes of Wrath,* Heinemann, 1939)

This map shows the places that Molly travelled to during
the three years she spent riding the boxcars of America.

For Ron and Moira

One

'Brother, Can You Spare a Dime?'

Once I built a railroad, I made it run,
Made it race against time.
Once I built a railroad,
Now it's done –
Brother, can you spare a dime?

Once I built a tower, up to the sun,
Brick and rivet and lime,
Once I built a tower,
Now it's done –
Brother, can you spare a dime?

Aunt Molly sang as she sewed. It was an old song the kids didn't know.

'What sorta song's that, Aunt Molly?' asked Danny.

'Oh, an old-time song. From way back, when I was a little girl.'

'What's it about?' Danny asked.

'The "Hard Times". This fella says: I built the railroads. I built that tower. I fought in the war. I worked hard for my country. Now I've nothing, no one gives a damn. I have to beg to survive. What went wrong?'

'Sing us some more,' pleaded Alice.

Aunt Molly put down her sewing, peered at her niece and nephew over her little round glasses and, in a cracked voice, began to sing once more.

Once in khaki suits,
Gee, we looked swell,
Full of that Yankee-doodle-de-dum.
Half a million boots went sloggin' through Hell,
And I was the kid with the drum!

Say don't you remember, they called me Al –
It was Al all the time.
Say don't you remember I'm your pal –
Buddy, can you spare a dime?

In the quiet that followed, the children stared at their aunt. Tears were rolling down her wrinkled face. It was Danny who broke the silence.

'Teacher's always telling us we should be glad to get

food and that, 'cause in the Great Depression people were starving, had no jobs, and all that stuff. Is it true?'

Aunt Molly wiped her eyes. 'Oh, yes. Nowadays, folks just go home, turn on the TV, watch a football game, go and fetch a glass of milk from the refrigerator, eat cookies. They couldn't do that in the thirties. No TV. Some had no home. And if they were hungry and there was nothing, they'd have to do without.'

'Did you ever go hungry, Aunt Molly?' asked Alice.

'Did I go hungry! There were times I'd faint from having nothing in my belly but air. Kids like me had to leave home and go wandering to find a job. I rode boxcars across America. They didn't call me 'Boxcar Molly' for nothing!'

'*Boxcar Molly!*' The children stared. 'Please tell us more,' they said.

Aunt Molly closed her eyes and rocked back in her chair. After a long pause, dredging up her memories, she began her story . . .

Two

The Seamstress

One day, I heard of jobs going at a knitwear factory in Oak Ridge. I was barely old enough to work – just fourteen. But it was getting more and more difficult for my family to make ends meet. I needed to spare my folks another mouth to feed. So the next morning, I got up at dawn to walk the three miles there. I could hardly believe my eyes when I saw hundreds of people crowded outside the factory gates. What were they all doing here? They knew there were only three or four jobs going.

Being small, I slipped to the front just as this big beefy guy came out. On either side, like bodyguards, were two cops.

'I need two girls for the seam machine,' the big guy shouted. 'Six cents a unit.'

A thousand people fought like a pack of huskies to get through the gates. I got swept forward in the surge, like driftwood on a tidal wave. Only *two* would get hired. The rush threw me up against the big man. He grabbed two arms, mine and another girl's, and yanked us through the gates.

We were in! Hired! It was my first job – seamstress in a knitwear factory.

Every morning, I got up at half past five. Tired and sleepy, I gulped down breakfast and set off for work. The mornings were chilly, but I knew it'd be hot at the mill. I started out on my three-mile walk. As I got closer, I'd see others hurrying to their jobs. I looked at the older folk and wondered if they, too, felt angry about their working conditions, or if, as the years went by, their spirits just died.

When I arrived at the factory, I saw the long line of jobless people waiting for the boss and hoping for work. That line seemed to get longer each day.

As I opened the door, a rush of hot steamy air greeted me. I hurried to my machine, as all the girls did, to get ready, so that when the whistle blew we could start work. Doing piece-work, every minute counted.

I seamed men's heavy underwear. With every twelve lots I got a stamp for six cents for large sizes, and only four cents for the smaller ones. At the end of the week, I pasted my stamps in a book and handed the book to the boss. He paid according to the number of stamps I had.

After I finished a dozen lots, I tied them up and carried them to the bin. The dozens were heavy, and grew heavier as the day wore on. The bin was usually full, and as I threw my dozen up on top, it often fell back down on me, knocking me over.

After finishing each dozen, tying it up, signing my number on the stamp, then carrying it to the next bin, I became so tired that my body and mind grew numb. Sometimes, to rouse myself, I went to the ladies' room. The toilet didn't flush. When I came to the water fountain, no matter how tired and numb I felt, I was always angry. The water was lukewarm, the fountain was rusty and filthy.

My lunch was usually spoiled. I could either put it on the bench where I kept my work and where it became squashed, or I could put it in a box under the bench and give the rats first choice.

On dull days, when it was almost time to go home, we took three minutes to put our coats on, then we stood in the aisles. All eyes would be on the boss, waiting for the signal. As soon as it came we rushed out.

I stuck it out for seven months. Then, one day as I was walking to work with seven cents and my lunch in my dungarees' pocket, I saw a truck heading out of town with its tailgate down. Goodness knows what came over me. I jumped on it and travelled all the way to some place called Bowling Green.

So there I was, wandering round this town looking for work. Everywhere was the same: 'We're firing, not hiring. Sorry, nothing doing here.' Hard times had come all right. After tramping the streets, I fell in with a crowd of kids all doing the same, and we finally headed for the railyard. The idea was to grab a freight train going somewhere – anywhere.

I soon learned that thousands of us were roaming the country, hopping freights, bumming food and living along the tracks in squatters' camps called 'jungles'. You sure grew up fast, if you survived at all, with these 'wild kids of the road'.

So there I was in the 'jungle', eating scraps and getting my first introduction to riding freight trains. My gang was planning to jump a train due out at midnight. What surprised me was the large number of females in the 'jungle'; some were girls, some women, and some mothers with babies. Many were dressed in slacks, so you could hardly tell if they were boys or girls.

I still had my seven cents, so I went with a couple of other kids to a nearby café for a hot drink. While I was getting some warmth into my bones, two women came in, one Mexican, one black. They ordered hamburgers. Then the guy behind the counter shouted, 'I don't serve niggers. Get that dame out of here!'

I'd never heard the like before. Why was black custom different from white? A cent's a cent, a dollar's a dollar, right?

Anyway, the women left. After a short while the Mexican woman came back and ordered two hamburgers. The guy grumbled, but fried up a couple. While he was busy, the black woman walked back in and sat down. Right away the guy dipped under the counter and came up with a baseball bat. Then he lashed out at her head. *Bong!*

Man, I thought he'd killed her. She groaned and staggered back off her stool. But the guy wasn't satisfied. With a roar, he cut round the corner, waving his bat. I stuck out my foot and tripped him up – he went sprawling on his face.

The women got out just in time, I reckon. We got out of there double-quick and grabbed the midnight freight for Atlanta, Georgia.

By luck we caught an orange freight and rode in the refrigerator car. That train went like a bat out of hell, jolting our insides into our mouths. All that separated us from the oranges was wire netting – we soon broke through the wire and ate as many oranges as we could. All that acid burnt my mouth and made my gums sore. By the time I got off at Greenville, South Carolina, I could hardly close my mouth. Not only that, I was tired and dirty from train smoke and cinders.

I slept in a tobacco warehouse with two other young tramps, one with a suitcase crammed with dirty clothes and a blanket smelling of mothballs. We hung around for a while, and then we bummed the town – going to different grocers and giving them our sob stories. We got a sausage here, bread or meat or can of beans there. Then we made for the railroad yard where we built a little fire and cooked up our food.

My first freight ride hadn't been much fun, so I thought I'd try the road next. In the morning I left town and turned south, walking the dusty track. It was cold, the wind smelt of winter. All day I went along steadily, getting the odd ride from trucks or Fords. When dinnertime came I asked for work at a farmhouse in exchange for food; and I picked peas with the farmer's family for a couple of hours.

That night I prised open a church window and slept on a wooden pew. It was either that or a tombstone in the graveyard!

For days I travelled across the country, making do as best I could, always on the lookout for food, work and a place to sleep. Eventually, I made my way to Charleston on the Atlantic seaboard in Southern Carolina. It was full of homeless kids from the North, brought there by false dreams of palm trees and warm sunshine. I slept two nights at the Salvation Army – the Sally. It was crowded with boys and young men, some with small bags, others with nothing at all. At the Sally, if you listened to a sermon, they'd feed you a little something. Once in a while somebody would claim they'd found religion. They'd stick around for a while, just to have a roof over their heads. But the first time they got enough money to get drunk, they did!

One boy, all rags and dirt, was so thin and far gone that even though us tramps were starving, we gave him food from our own stocks. That's how we were: we looked out for each other.

The third night I slept in the Charleston jail. The cops searched my clothes for weapons, my legs for knives or chains – thinking I might have escaped from a chain gang – and then showed me to a bench barely wide enough to sleep on.

Next day I grabbed a freight heading for Macon. Kids were scattered all over the train, with fifteen to twenty in the boxcar I was in. Some lay sleeping on old paper, others swapped stories, or passed on advice – of good places and friendly folk, and where to catch the trains in and out of big towns. We descended on Macon like a horde of locusts and bummed the streets and restaurants.

That night I left town and seemed to be the only one on the freight to Atlanta. Perhaps there were others, but this line had a bad reputation. Atlanta was a natural stop on the hobo route to the South. Anyone caught on a freight train in Fulton County got a thirty-day sentence in the city stockade or chain gang. So tramps tended to give it a wide berth.

I rode an oil tank and, as the night was cold, stood up, holding the railing with tight hands and staring ahead, watching the smoke grow red as the firemen stoked the boiler. I tied my bundle to the railing for fear of losing it, and stamped my feet to keep from dozing off. But, despite myself, I fell asleep. When I awoke with a start, I found myself leaning far over the grinding wheels. I was too scared to sleep for the rest of the night.

At each stop I noticed people, mainly black, getting on the train and throwing off coal. All along the tracks there were others, gathering it up. It wasn't long before a railway detective appeared on the roof and started getting tough, shouting at first, then shooting.

All at once, there he was with a flashlight that reached far into the night. *Bam! Bam!* I could hear the bullets hitting the car tops, just like in the movies. I threw up my hands and started walking towards the light.

The guy shouted, 'Get off!'

'I can't,' I replied. 'This thing's rolling too fast!'

He said, 'Jump!'

I said, 'I can't!'

He said, 'Turn around and march ahead.'

He marched me over the top. There was an open wagon about eight feet down. 'Jump,' he said.

So I jumped and landed in what felt like wet sand, up to my knees.

I thought my end had come. But the light grew dimmer and I was left, chilled to the bone, in the freezing sand. Early next morning the train crawled into a little town called Athens, and suddenly it was surrounded by deputies with pistols.

'I haven't done anything,' I said, pulling myself out of my hiding place.

They drove me and other tramps from the train to an old army warehouse. They checked us, separated boys from girls and made us take off our clothes to run them through a de-louser. When we came out, there was a spread with scrambled eggs, bacon, bread, coffee and toast. It was *wonderful*. Then we went upstairs to bed. There were sheets, toothbrushes, towels, everything. I sat down on my bed, full of amazement. I thought I'd gone to heaven.

Next day they shipped us out and told us not to come back again or we'd end up in the slammer.

Three

Riding the Railroad

You know what the Depression did to you? It made you a criminal, an outcast. You cheated, you lied, you got by, you survived any-old-how. You stole clothes off washing lines, you stole milk from people's doorsteps, you stole loaves of bread from shops.

I remember going through Memphis, Tennessee, on a freight. We made a short stop, no more than five minutes. Just across the track was this grocery store. I beat it off the train and just made it back as the train was moving out.

With a happy shout, I held up several rolls and cookies. I looked back to see this red-faced guy standing in the doorway of his store, shaking his fist and hollering loud enough to wake the dead.

They were rough times, all right. When I managed to get a job, I'd work from five in the morning till seven at night – washing dishes, peeling potatoes, cleaning floors, lugging heavy boxes and dumping garbage. Anything a grown man could do, I had to do just as well. The bosses made no allowance for age or sex.

When I got paid off, boy, I'd have to have my wits about me: with dough in your pocket you could get robbed and killed. I remember a kid named Scotty who was working down in the basement, firing the boiler in a big apartment block. Poor old Scotty worked so hard he was always sweaty and red from the heat. I felt so sorry for him. He was trying to send money home to his starving family. But other hoboes — mean, low-down murderers — killed him and tossed his body into the river! All for fifteen dollars! They'd have slit each other's throats for fifty cents.

If 1929 was hard, then 1930 was worse. I panhandled, begging for a nickel to buy something to eat. In the end, I decided to head for California. And I intended to travel in style on the *Santa Fe*. Open up those Golden Gates, California here I come . . .

There were whole families, even babies, crammed into one boxcar — fifty, maybe sixty people, all sprawled out on the floor. And if you wanted the toilet . . . too bad. You had to hold on till the next division point — usually about a hundred miles down the line.

One family stays in my memory as clear as if it were yesterday. The husband was very tall and haggard, and his wife was quite small with sunken cheeks from lack of food. With them were several children – the youngest was just a baby. The moment they entered the boxcar we all rallied round. We felt sorry for them and offered to share what food we had.

But that tall, lanky man was as stubborn as a mule. His pride got in the way of feeding his children. His baby was crying with hunger, yet he quietly and firmly said they didn't want anything to eat.

There was nothing we could do about it.

Anyway, we had to go through these mountains. The smoke from the stack of the engines and the soot were flying back through the tunnels and getting into the boxcars. So to avoid getting choked we bunged up the cracks with rags, and held handkerchiefs over our noses and mouths. True, we gave thought to the little baby. But the father told us not to worry – and to go ahead and keep out the soot.

When we emerged from the last tunnel, the baby seemed very still in its mother's arms. All at once, the mother let out a scream. And we realized that the baby had suffocated going through the tunnels. The whole boxcar grieved as if we'd lost one of our own.

So there I was, riding the *Santa Fe*. Not for me the plush seats and warm bed behind closed curtains. After the baby's death I took to the roof: four days and four nights in the open, with wind, smoke and cinders blowing in my face. Soon I was so hungry, cold and weak from lack of food, I started seeing long snakes crawling through the smoke. Next minute I was fast asleep – I couldn't help myself.

For sure I'd have fallen off the flyer into a cornfield; and the coyotes would have picked my bones clean. But as luck would have it this black hobo, a beanpole of a guy, wrapped his legs round me just as I was about to roll off the boxcar roof.

He saved my life.

Black or White, it didn't make any difference who you were. Everybody was poor. That put us all in the same boat. All were friendly, all slept in the jungle. We'd take a big pot and cook cabbage, meat and beans all together. We'd all live in a big makeshift tent. And when we rode the freight, some thirty of us would be on the railside, white and black together. We didn't have any mothers or fathers, brothers or sisters there to look out for us; we had no home. We were our own family, we were all we had – poor, dirty and starving.

We all had nicknames. That's how I came to be known as 'Boxcar Molly' – and it stuck. Another, a hellfire of a girl, was 'Fightin' Lil' – no one got the better of her. There were 'Hobo Hal', 'Texas Slim', and

'Big Chief Pow-Wow' – a real Indian chief. And there was 'Woody' Guthrie – he made it famous as a folk singer later. Young Woody was roaming his 'big green universe', as he called it. I remember him saying, 'We can sing you songs so full of hard travelling and hard sweating and hard fighting, you'll get big clear blisters in the palms of your hands just listening to us.'

He was always singing and playing his harmonica or guitar, composing songs for us and about us.

Anyways . . . This black guy who saved me went by the name of 'Beanpole'. He was two years older than me – sixteen. He'd never said more than two words to me before then. At first, trying to get him to talk more than a sentence at a time was hard work.

I found out, after asking a lot of questions, that Beanpole was a sharecroppers' child from Alabama. His father, mother and four other children old enough to be 'hands' all worked for the white landowner and were in debt to him.

I wanted to know more. 'Tell me what it was like,' I said.

Beanpole seemed surprised that anyone should take an interest in him. For a moment he was silent, then he slowly opened up and gave me a glimpse of a world I'd never imagined existed.

'I started picking cotton at the age of six, along with thousands of other kids. During the cotton-picking season my elder brother Tom pulled me out of bed at four o'clock – he was always quicker to hear the landlord's bell. Work on the plantation was always "from can see to can't see" – daybreak to dark—'

'But what about schooling?' I interrupted. 'Everyone has to be able to read and write.'

Beanpole didn't seem to like that question.

'I ain't stupid, Boxcar Molly! I went to school for three grades. Our black school ran for four months in the year – after the cotton-picking season ended. But then it was often too cold to go to school without shoes, so me and Tom took turns to walk there. We only had one pair of shoes between us.'

'I've never seen cotton-picking,' I said. 'It must be better than mining coal, like my pa did before the coughing sickness took him.'

Beanpole looked at me as if I didn't know anything.

'Some say coal's black gold and cotton's white gold. Black and white Hell, more like, for those who work on it! Picking cotton was back-breaking work in the summer heat. We worked a twelve-hour day, seven days a week, picking with both hands: pluck, pluck, drop-in-the-bag; pluck, pluck, drop-in-the-bag. It was easier when I was smaller because as I grew I had to stoop and move along on hands and knees. The cotton bolls grow all the way to the ground. So the pickers would be stooping, stooping all day long. As well as picking I had to drag along a big sack by a shoulder strap . . .'

Beanpole's family lived in a two-room cabin — all twelve of them. One small room was the kitchen and dining-room, the other was the bedroom and parlour. Meals consisted of 'white meat' and dry bread, 'white meat' being pork fat which cost only twenty-five cents a pound. It was all the family could afford.

Beanpole told me that the Depression didn't change much for the black folks: when the white man was low down, the black man was even lower! The only real change was that racists like those in the Ku Klux Klan blew the dust off their shotguns, whips and nooses. More and more blacks were being shot, whipped to death and lynched — not only do dead men tell no tales, they create jobs, too. White farm hands who'd left southern villages for better pay in the city five or six years earlier were now returning, out of work and stony broke. And they were demanding their old jobs back . . . Or else!

That meant a black school being burnt down in Graybridge, south-west Missouri, and a merchant in the town receiving a threatening note warning him to fire all his black employees . . . Or else!

Even on the trains, black railroad workers were being murdered because white railroadmen wanted their jobs. Beanpole knew of a fireman, Frank Kincaid, on the Mississippi division of the Illinois Central Railroad. Late one night he climbed into the cab of *The Creole* as crews were being changed at Canton, twenty-five miles north of Jackson. Against the lighted window he made a perfect target for a gunman hidden in the darkness outside.

A white man took his place, and *The Creole* pulled out for New Orleans.

One night, on the same division, fireman Ed Cole stepped down from his cab to throw a switch at Water Valley Junction. From behind the curtains of an unlit car that drew up beside the track a shotgun fired.

A white man took his place in the cab.

'Altogether,' Beanpole continued, 'in one year seven black railroad workers in Mississippi were shot dead, seven were wounded and one was flogged. No one was ever arrested. Murder wasn't news in Mississippi, and the killing of a black by a white man rarely reached the courts or even the pages of a newspaper.

'You see, Boxcar Molly, that's another sin of the Depression. It sets whites against blacks and it makes life even more dangerous for black people.'

Listening to Beanpole opened my eyes and ears to

what black folk had to suffer, especially in the southern states. No wonder in their songs and spirituals they sing of happiness that comes only when they're dead.

Four

Land of Milk and Honey

When Beanpole and I arrived in California, we joined the army. No, not with pack and rifle. The army of harvest hands and migrant workers. Those who followed the seasonal crops as pickers and dogsbodies. Here at last was work, at least for the season, till the trees and bushes were stripped bare. But it was also slavery for rock-bottom wages.

From July to October 1930, we picked figs at Fresno for the lordly sum of ten cents a box. For my fifteen boxes a day I earned one dollar and fifty cents.

From October to December we toiled in the vineyards near Fresno. No one could manage more than a six-hour day under the hot sun. I made twenty-five cents an hour – one dollar and fifty cents a day.

By now I was a wiry, tough fifteen-year-old, as brown as the figs I'd picked, my face roughened by sun and wind. Though I was still as skinny as a broom handle, my muscles were as hard and knotty as gnarled vines. My pal Beanpole cut my hair short with an old penknife – to give less houseroom to the creepy-crawlies who were always seeking a grimy, sweaty place to lay their eggs.

Come Christmas time the grapes were all done, sorted into table (Malaga) and wine (Muscat), and boxed ready to grace the tables of the rich. So our army upped and marched on to Imperial Valley where we pitched camp again. From February to March 1931, we picked peas – not as tasty as figs and grapes, but at least you didn't get belly ache all day long . . . Pay for all workers was the standard one cent a pound. I averaged a hundred and twenty-five pounds a day, for one dollar and twenty-five cents.

When the peas ran out, I worked as a 'wagon man' in a lettuce field. As the season got chillier, so did the wages: I was now getting sixty cents a day. I had to pay fifty cents a day for room and board.

'Room and board' sounds grand, doesn't it? Let me tell you what it was really like.

We took the main highway out of Fresno to Mendota, about thirty miles, then we turned west at Mendota for four miles. You couldn't miss it because of the big sign that read: *WELCOME TO THE LAND OF MILK AND HONEY.*

When we passed this sign we saw on the horizon a cluster of houses. This was the Hotchkiss Ranch – a comfortable farmhouse with barns and grape stores. We passed on by until we came to a row of fifteen tumbledown outhouses along the road. We couldn't miss them because of the stink and the swarms of flies that hovered above them.

This was a typical migrant workers' camp. Some had five outhouses for workers, some thirty. It all depended on the size of the farm. My 'lodgings' were in an outhouse where a baby girl had scarlet fever. She slept on an iron bedstead, while her mother tried to shoo the flies away. That was the *only* bed and it was one of only five in the whole camp. The other six in this family, as well as I, slept huddled together: father, mother, two grown boys, a little boy and a teenage girl. We slept like almost everyone else in the camp – on the floor.

The barrel and rusty milk can in the corner of our room held the water we brought from Mendota to cool the child's fever. It was four miles to Mendota and four miles back, so we had to be very sparing with the water. That's why we all looked so dirty – not because we didn't like to wash. It was because water was needed for cooking and drinking. You couldn't waste water just washing yourself when it took so long to get.

The young girl of the family looked thin and tired.

I noticed she was pregnant. She told me she was only fifteen. When I asked her how long she'd been working in the fields she shrugged her shoulders. 'Dunno. Maybe eight. Maybe nine when I started. I dunno.'

Tough, eh?

It was now 1931. Early March was the slack time, right up to June when the fruit-picking season started again. Beanpole and I decided to try our luck on the San Francisco waterfront. Nothing doing. There were a thousand people or more at five in the morning, all chasing four jobs.

We had this crazy idea of going to sea. Of course we had no ticket. We just stood on the docks, watching those great old liners that sailed to Hawaii. You could hear the band playing *Aloha Away*, and there we all were with tears in our eyes, as if we knew somebody going some place . . . Yet we didn't know a soul!

When we found no jobs on the waterfront, we'd drift up to Skid Row where thousands would be swarming around. Guys stood on boxes – socialists, communists, anarchists – making strange speeches.

One leader would say, 'Let's go to City Hall.' And we'd all troop off, singing songs and chanting, 'We want work! We demand shelter for our families! We want food!' That sort of thing. On the steps of City Hall, there'd be more speeches. I remember how brave this seemed to me – all those bold demands.

One time thirteen families, victims of a recent fire, took over an empty three-storey apartment block, defying the police to evict them.

Mrs Pearl Moore, Tenants' Union representative, declared, 'Man, we're going to stake out those apartments just like the early settlers when they took land away from the Indians!'

We knew society wasn't going to give us anything. But we protested all the same. At City Hall, the mayor came out, mouthed off and told us nothing. He was Angelo Rossi, a little Italian immigrant. He wore a tight cherry waistcoat over his bulging stomach, and expensive boots with built-up heels to make himself look bigger.

After City Hall, the guys who'd made the speeches led us on a parade round town. There were so many of us on the parade it snaked back four blocks, curb to curb. None of us had a dime. Yet there were guys on corners trying to sell us apples and matches!

As we arrived in the city centre, we ran into cops on horses – they used to have cops on horses in those days. That's when the fighting started. It got real rough because some guys had brought along a bunch of marbles and began to roll them down the street under the horses' hooves. That made those horses slip and slide all over the place, dumping cops on the ground. They didn't like that, it made them mad. I heard later that three protesters were shot dead that day.

We never expected to win. Generally we were a gentle crowd, just kids and fathers. We didn't want to kick society to pieces. We weren't talking revolution. We just wanted to work and couldn't understand why there were no jobs. We felt bewilderment, not anger.

I had no idea what it was all about until I went back to Los Angeles and ran into this little guy by the name of Upton Sinclair. He was speaking at a meeting. He talked about the great piles of oranges and the heaps of lumber lying idle. Food was being destroyed to keep the prices up, while we went hungry.

Sinclair's idea was simple: this food should be eaten up by hungry people instead of being guarded by men with guns while it rotted.

Sinclair was running for Governor of California in 1931. His slogan was EPIC – END POVERTY IN CALIFORNIA. Beanpole and I joined his campaign. At this time I would look for work in the early morning, give up at around eleven and drift into the library where I'd pick up books I'd never seen before. That was my routine. I got my education there really. Many of us spent our free time reading, especially radical newspapers that opened our eyes to the senselessness and the injustices around us.

If I had to pick a constant enemy during that time, it was the American Legion. I couldn't understand why they didn't want us to use the library and read. And they really had it in for Beanpole. They seemed to think that black people had no business reading books and newspapers. In their view, reading and education gave black folks thoughts they'd no right to.

These American Legionnaires hated us. The very sight of us seemed to offend their sense of decency. Every place I went – the railroad yards, the Hoovervilles, the protest meetings – they raided. They'd arrive wearing baseball caps, holding clubs or bats in their hands, shouting and screaming.

Sinclair's campaign for Governor drove them crazy. They'd descend on his meetings to break them up. Once, they crept up on us, cracking heads and beating us up. We barely escaped alive.

The American Legionnaires were the 'Main Streeters', people doing all right in the Depression – merchants, storekeepers, landowners. They were terrified of revolution. A lot of businesspeople were expecting it. The government sent out spies to the Hoovervilles and railroad yards, collecting information on what people were saying and thinking.

The message they sent back was: 'Revolution!' The spies claimed that people were talking revolution all over the place. They said that guys riding the freight trains were talking about what they'd like to do with a machine gun, how they'd like to tear loose on the rich. They reported that people were eagerly reading socialist and communist publications, having good old crackerbarrel discussions.

If any of this revolution stuff was true, I never came across it. Maybe the spies made it up to keep themselves in a job. But all the rumours flying around made people jittery, especially the government and police. The cops had a way of dealing with anyone they regarded as a 'troublemaker'. And what they did to troublemakers never got published in the papers.

Let me give you an example. There was a police detail in Chicago known as the 'Red Squad'. It was led by a roughneck lieutenant by the name of Mike Mills. When a strike occurred, Mills would arrange with the factory bosses to arrest the leaders. Mills and his men would beat them up, put them in jail and make it clear that they'd better get the hell out of town.

Sometimes Mills would go into a saloon with his plainclothes men – they'd be tipped off that the leaders were having a quiet drink there. All at once, a fight'd break out and the cops would set upon these 'red agitators', sling them in jail and then kick them out of town.

There was a lot of rough stuff going on that ordinary folk never got to hear about.

Probably the worst happened on the last Monday in May, Memorial Day. A few days before, some steel workers had picketed Republic Steel in the far south of Chicago. They'd got clobbered and ended up with a few split skulls. That made the workers mad. So they organized a big demonstration on Memorial Day. A few came looking for trouble, but for most it was simply a family picnic sort of holiday: there were little kids, people dressed up in their Sunday shirts, that sort of thing. Many just came for the fun of it; they weren't expecting any trouble.

The police were standing in line in front of Republic Steel, quite a distance from the demonstrators. It was a really hot day, about ninety degrees. They had their winter uniforms on. The sun was strong, and all I could see were stars on their shoulders glittering. Nobody was armed. But the police got the idea that these people were. At least, they were told so by Captain Mooney, who was managing the whole operation.

I held back as the crowd moved on. All of a sudden, I heard some popping going on and saw a blue haze rising.

It was tear gas.

About three minutes later, the ambulances started bringing in the wounded. About fifty people were shot. Ten people died.

I was in the gallery of the court when the case was heard a few days later. The assistant state's attorney asked the doctor who had attended the victims, Dr Lewis Andreas, where the dead and wounded were shot.

'Most were shot in the back,' he said.

'Can you define "the back?" ' was the next question.

Dr Andreas got up and turned around, saying, 'What you're looking at now − that's the back.'

Most people in the courtroom laughed at that, but the police and judge weren't amused. An eyewitness said that a few rocks had been thrown at the police before the shooting started. Then the protesters all turned and ran. As they were running the police shot them.

The police weren't all bad. Some of them quit the force because of what had happened. Of course, the newspapers turned the whole thing on its head. After all, the wealthy newspaper owners supported law and order, as long as it was *their* order. There was a picture on the back page of *The Tribune*: a little old guy lying in the road in his white shirt, blood streaming down his face and a policeman beating the hell out of him with his club. The caption told a different story: *Striker Beats Up Police at Republic Steel Riot.*

It wasn't just the police that enforced 'law and order'. When demonstrations affected local newspapers, they hired their own thugs to deal with the protestors. The Hearst morning newspaper, *The Herald Examiner*, was suffering a long strike at this time. Outside the newspaper building journalists were picketing. Now, the Hearst delivery trucks were manned by delivery men who doubled up as armed thugs. One day in Chicago I saw this pale, bloodied reporter lying on the pavement as colleagues and passers-by stared in horror. In the middle of the street stood a squat thug with a car jack in his hand, arms and legs apart, challenging all comers. Of course, the police just stood by, looking on.

Five

Breaking the Law

When times got really hard in Chicago at the back end of '31, Beanpole and I scrounged a corner of a flat. Everyone in the neighbourhood was out of work and hard up. We got by as best we could, cheating on gas and electricity. When the gas or electricity company found out, they'd come and take out the meter. But there was this guy in the next block who'd rig up a 'jumper' wire so that the current went around the meter instead of through it.

For many folks it was either break the law or break your back, watching the kids starve to death or die of cold.

As far as I was concerned, the law only protected the rich and, in any case, the cops were all crooked. Beanpole, however, would rather live rough than risk a serious brush with the law. He didn't mind riding freight or minor panhandling, but crossing swords with the utilities was too much.

'It's all very well for you white folks,' he'd say. 'If a black guy gets caught, the cops send him down for a long stretch or get the hit squad to pepper him full of lead.'

'But we have to survive,' I'd argue.

'We *must* obey the law,' he'd insist.

A real straight-down-the-middle, law-abiding fellow, he was – he had to be. In the end, I gave in and decided to 'go straight'. I accompanied Beanpole to the Hooverville on the edge of town; it was reasonably safe if you were down-and-out. Here, people lived in old, rusted car bodies, or shacks made of orange crates. There was one family with a whole tribe of kids living in a piano box. This Hooverville wasn't just a tiny cluster of slum shacks, it was maybe ten miles wide by ten miles long.

For food we stood in the bread and soup lines with other hopeless cases. Most would just take what was given, however useless. Beanpole was a bit like that. I had to teach him to speak up for himself. If he happened to be one of the first people in the soup line, he got nothing but the greasy water at the top. So I forced Beanpole to ask the guy ladling out the soup into our tin bowls – we all had to bring our own bowls – to dip down for some meat and potatoes at the bottom.

'And if he won't do it,' I told Beanpole sternly, 'get

mad and say: "Dip down, Goddamn it!" '

I think the worst thing that the Depression did to people was to take away their pride, their human dignity. I remember seeing an elderly man standing on a deserted corner near the vast, idle Everett Mills plant. He was just standing there like an undotted question mark, unaware of me watching him.

He was mumbling to himself. Then all at once he stepped off the curb and picked up a long piece of string from a pile of rubbish. His big, work-hungry hands went into action, tying and untying it. He worked with the string for several minutes. Then he looked round and, seeing me, dropped the string, his long thin face colouring a little.

For a few seconds he stood looking down at the rubbish heap, then up at me, as if he wanted to explain. Finally, he turned round, hesitated a moment as if he didn't know where to go, and shuffled off. His overcoat was split down the back and the heels of his shoes were completely worn away.

When Beanpole and I were really starving we used to eat wild greens from the fields, what we called 'hobo salad' – violet tops, wild onions, forget-me-nots and dandelion leaves. You had to take care not to eat poisonous weeds, or you'd end up with a stomach ache.

So we learned to eat only what the cows ate; they could be relied on never to touch dangerous weeds.

Of course, I felt shame. I didn't like people seeing me dirty and raggedy, all skin and bone. Despite taking care over eating weeds and tree bark, I finally took sick and couldn't eat for two or three days. If it hadn't been for Beanpole, I might well have been done for. He did what he could to look after me, spooning soup into my mouth and keeping me warm.

Only when I recovered did I really come to appreciate all he'd done.

'You saved my life again, Beanpole,' I told him.

'You'd do the same for me,' he mumbled.

I thought about that. Yes, I suppose I would. I hadn't given much thought to Beanpole in that light before. Now I realized that neither of us was really on our own any more. I could rely on Beanpole, and he could rely on me.

'You're the only person, the *only* person, who cares what happens to me,' I said.

Beanpole didn't speak for a while; he just stared down at his dirty, cracked fingernails.

'Well,' he said at last, 'we're friends, aren't we, Molly?'

I looked at his creased forehead, his weary eyes and his skinny arms – he was a real bag of bones. And I

36

suddenly realized that he'd starved himself to feed me. Fondness for him filled my heart. Oh, Beanpole! For the first time in my life I felt genuine affection for someone.

I lent over and kissed him lightly on the cheek. 'Thank you,' I said.

Six

No Hope

A chill wind began to blow through the Windy City, as Chicago was called. No work. No home. No hope. The cloud hanging over our Hooverville colony was black with depression and Depression. And it wasn't shifting. If ever jobs opened in some place, word would go round the hovels. A hobo would tell his buddies: 'Detroit, no jobs. Pittsburgh, no jobs. They're hiring in New York.'

And the word would spread like wildfire through the dead wood of our jungle. The next train heading east would be teeming with hopeful no-hopers.

By now Beanpole and I were real down-and-outers. We were prepared to try anything. Beanpole had remembered the address of an uncle living in the big city. He'd moved out of the southern cotton fields, like many African Americans, when the boll weevil had moved in. That pesky little beetle had ruined vast acres of land. As a result, many black sharecroppers and field hands, cut off from credit, cold and hungry in their tumbledown shacks, had no place to turn ... except North.

That way lay the promise of jobs, homes, schools and freedom from want. As the Depression went on, they also faced increased terror from the Ku Klux Klan in the South. So, with the dream of '*Jesus will lead me, Welfare will feed me,*' they trekked north – to Detroit, Michigan, Pittsburgh, New York.

What they didn't anticipate was that, after the Crash, the one-industry cities, employing steel or car workers, would be ruined. And, as the old saying goes, blacks were 'the last hired and first fired'.

Beanpole and I had no idea of this disaster awaiting us; we were just fired up with a burning desire to quit Chicago and park ourselves on Beanpole's uncle in New York. Something was bound to turn up!

But first we had to get to New York – which was easier said than done. As I was saying, hundreds of hoboes had the same idea once this guy had whispered 'jobs' in the ear of his buddy. The trouble was the railroad police. They were mean; they were so mean they'd pour water on a drowning man! We heard that they'd shoot people off the trains. No questions asked. Just yank open a freight door and fire: *bang-bang-bang*, sweeping all four corners.

But what had we to lose? Only our worthless lives. Who would be there to mourn us when we were gone? The prize, however, if you made it, was a good job and a good home . . . So we chanced it. But *not* in a boxcar – just in case trigger-happy cops were out to clean the place with hobo blood. To be on the safe side, we'd ride on top despite the wind and cold. Even so, the railroad cops had heard what was going on. They suddenly descended on the railroad yards and stations whenever a freight train moved out.

Our best bet, we figured, was to hide in the long trackside grass at a bend just out of town. As the freight train slowed down, we'd leap aboard and clamber up to the roof before anyone could stop us. At night they wouldn't spot us anyway.

Beanpole and I weren't the only ones in on the plan. There must have been a hundred or more, mostly kids like us, crouching in the grass as night fell. It was raining, a cold drizzle that chilled us to the bone. Someone was playing a harmonica, a dismal spiritual that just about summed up our mood.

All at once, the shadows started flitting about as we caught the distant chuff-chuff of the train; then came a low, long, mournful whistle. And the old Chesapeake and Ohio Railway, the C & O, came chugging down the line, clickety-clack, clickety-clack. As expected, it slowed down for the bend. That was our chance.

'Go, man, go!' someone yelled.

In a bumping, shoving mass we all leapt out of the wet grass towards the narrow corridors between freight wagons.

Beanpole grabbed a rail and hauled himself up, panting and sticking out an arm to pull me on board. 'Yippee!' I shouted. We'd made it. Almost at once, my joyful cry stuck in my throat like a fishbone. The young boy behind me slipped on the greasy footstep and, with a sharp scream, disappeared under the wagon wheels. Clickety-clack, clickety-clack.

We had no time to grieve. At least that poor kid didn't have to sit with us on the boxcar roof in the driving rain and sleet, huddled together against the cold, hanging on like grim death to the wet rail and remembering to duck down at each tunnel – or end up headless. It would be like this for the next hundred miles until the next stop – Detroit.

Detroit. Good old motor town – Motown. Centre of the US automobile industry: Ford, Chrysler, General Motors, Dodge. A busy, bustling city full of smoke and honest grime.

Well, not any more.

It was early morning and the freight train had ground to a halt in a goodsyard. We had a few hours before it reloaded and moved on out for Buffalo. It gave us an opportunity to stretch our legs, to get the blood sloshing around our frozen bodies, reaching numbed feet and hands. Maybe Dodge or Chevrolet were hiring?

They weren't.

In the trackside jungle we met up with a one-time auto worker, Lewis, who gave us the low-down on the 'employment situation'.

'Nobody's buying autos any more,' he said. 'So no one's making them.' With a deep sigh, he added, 'My feet's real sore.'

Lewis had been tramping all over town looking for work, anything to help feed his six young kids. His shoes, one brown, one black, were cracked and split, the soles having parted company from the uppers. The wind blew up from the river in icy gusts, chilling us all to the marrow through our threadbare clothing. Lewis didn't even have an overcoat.

He showed us round, just to do something and keep on the move. We passed about two hundred men huddled together across the road from the Ford Rouge employment office.

'They're all former Ford workers,' Lewis said, 'most laid off in 1929. More than two years on, they're still hoping that Ford will start hiring again.'

The three of us walked on for a few more miles to the

Fleetwood plant of Fisher, the biggest car-body plant in the world – that was their boast before the Crash came. Again the employment office was packed with listless men and women. On to Chevrolet. Now we were tramping through falling snow. The snow made the cold even colder. In front of the L.A.Young plant a dozen boys were crowded together, the oldest was about fifteen. They looked as if they'd been there all night. Pale and cold and sleepy, they cowered in the biting wind. They followed us with hostile glares as we hurried on.

Outside the Dodge plant, the men made their feelings known to us. Their insults were mainly directed at Beanpole.

'Keep moving, coloured boy,' a burly fellow shouted. 'Don't come sniffing round here for work.'

The cry seemed to stoke up more resentment and stir others to life. 'Blackleg niggers! They take our jobs at starvation wages!'

A low murmur of sullen agreement passed through the crowd. Someone else bawled, 'Get back to the South where you belong!'

Beanpole said nothing, just hung his head and quickened his pace. But it made my blood boil. Didn't these men see what they were doing? The Depression was turning one worker against another. Fear bred hatred. I wasn't going to stand for that.

I marched straight over to the crowd and shouted at them, 'Shame on you! Don't you see? This is what the bosses want: worker against worker, black against white. That way you don't blame the system. If there were no black people, who'd you blame then? Irish? Poles? Women? We're *all* Americans. We have to stand together.'

It was the first time I'd ever addressed a crowd. Perhaps it was because I was a girl that they went quiet; no one attacked me. In fact, a few voices supported me.

'She's right.'

'You tell 'em, gal!'

'Black and white together!'

Lewis hissed in my ear, 'Come away. The mood could turn nasty.'

He was right. I'd stirred up a hornet's nest. A couple of scuffles broke out as we were turning the corner.

Once we'd said goodbye to Lewis, Beanpole took my hand and squeezed it, muttering, 'Thanks for sticking up for me, Molly.'

I said nothing, just smiled up at him. Little was I to know how soon he would have to do the same for me.

We were passing the Hamtramck plant of Briggs Body, which was all boarded up, when we caught up with a steady line of men and women, tramping away from it towards Murray Body. For some reason women were everywhere on the road. Young and old, women with kids in tow, pregnant women. Just one continuous stream passing along, looking for jobs.

Beanpole and I tagged on to the long line. At the Murray Plant, there were no jobs. But former workers were allowed to sign their names on a list – they'd get priority when 'the good times' came again. At first, I wasn't aware of this and stood in line to sign the list.

'Have you worked here, lady?' the superintendent asked.

'No, but I'm able and willing,' I said.

He turned to some men behind him. 'She's able and willing!' he sneered.

'Oh, is she?' said a man with a leer. 'Then we'll have to give her a good seeing to.'

The rest laughed loudly.

'That's what a woman's for,' called another man. 'They're not fit for our work.'

A few made wolf-whistles and crude gestures.

I went as red as a beetroot, too ashamed to say anything. But Beanpole's face turned pale. Before I could stop him, he strode forward and snatched the list from the man's hands, tearing it into pieces.

The red-faced bully wasn't going to be insulted by a

black boy. With one blow from his meaty fist, he knocked Beanpole to the ground.

'A lady's man, huh?' he yelled. 'Myself, I'm a man's man.'

Beanpole slowly got to his feet, blood streaming from his nose and split lip. Unsteady on his spindly legs, he raised his fists like a boxer and muttered, 'You aren't a man, you're a coward. Apologize to my friend or put your mitts up.'

Urged on by his cheering friends, the big fellow swung another punch at Beanpole's head. This time Beanpole dodged out of the way. The man was off balance and Beanpole hit him in the midriff, doubling him up.

'Come on, Gerry,' shouted someone. 'Knock the kid out.'

But Gerry was wary now. He circled Beanpole, sizing him up and waiting for an opening. Beanpole got in some jabs to the ear and nose, but they just bounced off the bully's face. When he realized that this black kid had more courage than skill, he waded in with flailing arms. One blow was bound to hit the target.

This time Beanpole did not get up.

I rushed to his side, brushing the dirt off him and wiping away the blood with my headscarf. As I was tending to him, some of the women bystanders set on the bully with their umbrellas, telling him what they thought of him. When he saw that his pals were no longer behind him, he turned tail and ran off.

'Come on, girl,' said a young woman to me. 'Let's clean him up.'

She helped me raise Beanpole to his feet. And with us acting as crutches beneath his armpits, he staggered down to a houseboat by the lakeside where cold water soon brought him round. His first words were, 'Thanks, Molly. One good turn deserves another.'

We managed to drag Beanpole on to a rickety old houseboat and forced some hot tea down his throat. With that he passed out again and I let him sleep.

I'd noticed that my helper, though as ragged and dirty as us, had airs and graces she couldn't quite hide. She was young, no more than sixteen, I'd guess. While Beanpole was resting, she told me she came from a family of teachers. But the school suddenly stopped paying them and eventually they got laid off. The whole school went on strike in protest.

'We all went down to City Hall to protest' she continued. 'And what happened? I saw unpaid policemen cracking the heads of unpaid schoolteachers. That's education for you!

'After that debt collectors hunted us down. We had no fire to keep warm by, the lights were cut off; they came and cut off the water. Every now and then my brother or father would find some sort of odd job, or my eldest brother in Detroit would send us a little something. Then we'd go wild over food. We'd eat until we were sick. We just couldn't help ourselves. But most times we starved, like other families.'

Evidently, she'd come to Detroit to seek help from her brother. But she was going home empty-handed.

By the time Beanpole and I reboarded the freight train, we were glad to get away from the depressing scene. But in Buffalo and Pittsburgh the situation was even worse. By now our hopes of finding work in New York were beginning to fade. If over half the population of the cities we'd passed through were out of work, they would surely have crowded into New York. After all, the nation's largest city had the nation's biggest hotels, tallest skyscrapers, richest mansions, busiest stock exchange . . .

All at once we sighted the distant skyscrapers of Brooklyn and Staten Island. Despite the gloom it was an exciting moment.

'New York, New York, what a wonderful town!' we sang.

Seven

New York

That afternoon in the winter of 1931, New York gave us a chilly welcome. It seemed too cold to rain; but it wasn't. The drops came down in slanting lines, driven by a bitter wind. The rainwater stood in pools upon the railroad yard and along the shining streets.

Hands deep in pockets, collars high up around ears, we headed for the Bowery where we'd heard there was a lodging house for the homeless. Beanpole had no idea if his uncle had received his letter informing him of our little social visit.

'We'll wait a couple of days and see how the land lies before we drop in on him,' Beanpole said.

We had heard that five nights per month was the limit allowed at the Municipal Lodging House run by the New York City Department of Public Welfare. So we hoped for five nights' board until we descended on

Beanpole's uncle. I couldn't help wondering if he would welcome visitors.

We headed for the lodging house, down on 25th Street near the East River. It wasn't hard to find. As we approached the Bowery we began to see little knots of people huddled in doorways or under bridges with the trains rumbling overhead. What with the rain and freezing wind, it was a bad time to be out, even if you were warmly dressed. These people weren't. Their shoes were broken, their clothes threadbare. They stared at us as we passed.

Now and then a joker had assembled half a dozen or more people about him. They would laugh noisily, unnaturally, whenever he reached the punch-line of the joke. For most of the crowd, this was the only sound they made. These people were frightened; and frightened people keep silent.

Uneasily, Beanpole and I passed them by and turned a corner. We stopped dead in our tracks. Before us was a long line of men and women, three or sometimes four abreast, a block long, and wedged tightly together, so tightly that no one could get by.

I turned to Beanpole. 'What's this about?' I asked.

'I guess that those at the front will eat tonight; and those at the back probably won't.'

He was right. Every few minutes someone tried to

break in at the front. From behind came a chorus of boos and jeers: the hungry and homeless disapproved of line jumpers.

Beanpole and I joined the line and got chatting to a middle-aged, barrel-chested man in front of us. He turned out to be an old hand at standing in line.

'The lodging house opens at four in the afternoon,' he said in a deep growl; 'so we've an hour to kill before the line starts moving. It'll be twice as long by six. They take in one-hundred-and-twenty-eight – not a single body more or less – every twenty-five minutes. That's the length of time it takes for one sitting in the dining-room.'

'What sort of grub do they serve up?' I asked.

'Each person gets a cup of coffee (in a tin mug, boiling hot), a big dish of stew (beef tonight, lamb tomorrow) and as much bread as they can eat. Anyone capable of downing a second helping of stew is welcome to it.'

Our bellies started to rumble at the thought of it. As much food as we could eat!

'God, I'd sleep for ever after a meal like that,' said Beanpole with a grin.

'Me, I'm only here for the food,' said our friend. 'But if you want to stay the night, you're allowed eleven hours' sleep.'

'What happens if you don't get into the lodging?' asked Beanpole.

We were beginning to think the unthinkable: that we wouldn't make it that night.

'There are a few flophouses. And, of course, there's always the Salvation Army if you don't mind an ear-bashing from bible-punchers. But there aren't nearly enough beds to go round.'

'So where do people who don't get in go?' I asked, fearing I might find out pretty soon anyway.

'Oh, they take in the city, walking about its squares and parks,' he said with a wry smile. 'It's a grand place, full of statues and bright lights: Times Square, Broadway, the Empire State Building, Central Park. Best of all are the public libraries – grand institutions for improving the mind, and warming the soul and seat of your pants! The only drawback is that there's nowhere to go when the libraries shut . . .'

As he was speaking, the line started to move, and everyone came to life.

'Don't lose your place,' warned our new friend.

He need hardly have bothered. The line edged forward at a snail's pace. Four o'clock came and went. Six o'clock. Eight o'clock. We were still half a block away from food and board when the line stopped moving, and people began to drift away with slouched shoulders and a stiff walk.

'What happens now?' I asked the big fellow.

'What happens? We walk the streets. If you smoke, you gather up cigarette ends or cigar butts from the pavement. Or you can rummage in refuse cans for discarded newspapers and other rubbish. You never know what you might find. And when all else fails, you bum. Trouble is, you're competing with a few thousand other beggars.'

I looked blankly at Beanpole. Our friend wandered off into the night and we stood alone on the pavement. But all at once he turned back and beckoned us to follow him. We fell in behind, as if following the Pied Piper.

'I'll take you to the soup line,' he said. 'At least you'll get a hunk of bread and a bowl of soup to tide you over till tomorrow. And tomorrow, as they say, is another day. The soup-kitchen closes at nine; if we hurry we might just make it in time.'

We trotted after him through once-vacant parking lots near the water's edge, in the swamps of the New Jersey side of the Hudson River. This derelict area was now full of shanty towns made from tin cans and packing boxes. It housed thousands of idle workers. Finally, at the north end of Central Park we came to yet another line of hungry people waiting patiently in the bitter wind for a turn at the soup counter.

Thanks to a couple of bossy cops shouting, 'Move along there!' and, 'Come on, hurry it up!' we soon reached the front and gratefully accepted our soup and bread.

As we squatted down on some packing boxes to swallow and slurp our only meal of the day, our friend cheered us up with a little tale.

'One day I picked up an old copy of the *New York Herald Tribune*. It ran a story about this restaurant offering bargain meals: *ALL YOU CAN EAT FOR SIXTY CENTS*.

'Now, I didn't have two nickels to rub together. But this rough-looking guy went into the restaurant one Friday night, sat at a table and slapped down his sixty cents. He ordered a tomato-juice cocktail, soup, three portions of liver with onions and potatoes, two salads, four cups of coffee, a pie à la mode, a custard, and some other desert, and a watermelon (whole). For bread he had crackers, corn muffins and wholewheat rolls. He could hardly get through the door when he left!'

The description of all that food made our mouths water. I shut tight my eyes and imagined the soup was really liver with onions and potatoes, and that the bread was corn muffins. What the hell! It filled a space. Who cares what it tasted like?

'Tell you what, swells.' It was our buddy who interrupted my feast. 'Why don't you come over to my place? Nothing grand, mind you, but it's warm and cosy.'

He looked at us from under his great coarse eyebrows, his big seamed face full of honest sincerity.

'An honour and a pleasure,' I said with a mock bow.

We set off through the dark, damp streets for his Hooverville property. It was just at the foot of East 10th Street. The estate had a hundred or so dwellings, though each 'home' was no bigger than a dog house or chicken coop, made skilfully from wooden crates, metal cans, strips of cardboard and old tar paper. Here people lived by collecting garbage and all sorts of junk. Some stood outside their 'homes', splitting and sawing wood with dull tools to make fires. Others were picking through heaps of rubbish piled in front of their doorways or cooking over open fires or battered oilstoves. As they went about their business, they paid no attention to us or the slum children playing underfoot.

We finally came to a shack clinging to the shore like a barnacle. A sign was scrawled on a plank above the low door: *Abandon hope, all ye who enter here!*

Our friend's 'house' was almost filled by the three of us. But he sat Beanpole and me down on two wooden boxes as he got a fire going inside his hearth of bricks – that was his stove – on which he perched a lidless kettle. He lit a lamp slanting from a spike in the wall; it coughed and spluttered with the last drops of oil. A narrow plank bed filled the whole of the back end and a small shaky table ran along one side.

He introduced himself: 'Delaney.' No first name.

'I'm from Ireland,' he said. 'But I'm American, a Yankee-doodle Dandy. Thirty years I've been in this country. And I fought for it in the war, you know.'

He spoke the last two words angrily. As if ashamed of his slight outburst, he changed the subject.

'Sometimes I can get bread from the bakeries. It's a day or two old, maybe, but it's OK to eat and they can't sell it any more. That's what we do, visit the small stores, getting food that would rot anyway. But coffee and sugar, tobacco and oil for the lamp, or kerosene for a stove – those are the things that are hard to get.'

Only a few years ago, it turned out, Delaney had been a contractor in the building trade, in a small way. He showed us a picture of his wife and their three-year-old son.

'They're still with her folks,' he said miserably. 'If I do make any dough, I try to send some of it, but hell . . .' He shrugged his shoulders and raised his hands to the ceiling just above his head.

We drank some weak coffee. New York hadn't turned out to be exactly what Beanpole and I had expected. In fact, at first sight it seemed to be the capital of all the nation's misery. What made New York different was the ugly sight of so much wealth next to so much poverty.

Eight

Uncle Henry

Beanpole and I stayed just one night with Delaney. It wasn't fair to burden him any longer. Not only that, there wasn't room to swing a cat in his shack. And although I slept on the rickety table covered in newspapers, poor Beanpole found no room for his long legs on the floor; he ended up with one foot on the bottom shelf and one under Delaney's bed.

After thanking him for his kindness, Beanpole and I went in search of our only contact in New York — Beanpole's uncle. The address was a tenement east of Lenox Avenue.

It was painfully evident even before we located the apartment block that we were descending into the depths of hell. The building we were seeking loomed blackly on the corner of its block: seven storeys, thick dark windows, caged in a dingy nest of fire escapes, hunched up and jam-packed with wriggling life.

At one time it had been a grand hotel. Now, in the dim little entrance hall, the peeling plaster and broken fancy grille of the elevator hinted at better times – and showed just how low the one-time hotel had fallen.

The whole place was in darkness. We discovered that the tenants could not afford to pay for light. Or heating. The place was as cold as death. To add to the squalor and cold, the building had been condemned by the local authorities after a fire had killed a dozen people.

Since it wasn't any good for anything else, the owner had turned it over to the poorest of the poor: the city's black people – those who were in no position to object to the fire hazard, the dark and the cold. They were crammed into the hotel, getting along as best they could.

'Does your uncle live *here?*' I asked Beanpole, wide-eyed.

'The last we heard, Molly,' he said, 'Uncle Henry had made it big. He was a veteran of the Great War, then he became foreman of the Sunkist Pie Company. Somehow I expected a big house in a leafy suburb.'

Our hopes were swiftly fading.

It wasn't hard to track down Beanpole's uncle. A tenant in the entrance hall gave us directions down into the basement below street level.

If it was dingy above ground, down below it was pitch black. Carefully, we felt our way down a flight of stone steps into a maze of cellars. This had once been a vast underground basement housing the central heating system, even providing a parking lot for hotel residents. Now it had been converted into makeshift apartments — cells would have been a better description. All that separated them were flimsy cardboard walls.

The underground people were packed into these damp, rat-ridden dungeons — one room per family. Floors were cracked concrete, side walls were whitewashed rock, water-drenched and rust-streaked. And, of course, there were no toilets.

We were guided to Beanpole's uncle in the distant corner of the basement — still unable to credit what we were seeing . . . or smelling! However, Uncle Henry was surprisingly cheerful. He shared the makeshift room with his widowed mother. A tall grizzled man, he shook our hands warmly and invited us in. For light he was burning a kerosene lamp, and for warmth a small coal stove.

Straight away, we noticed that the room had no furniture — just cardboard spread on the concrete floor for bedding. Uncle Henry explained that before he'd lost his job (it had gone to a white man half his age) he'd purchased a suite of furniture for two-hundred-and-eighty-five dollars, and he'd paid off all but the last instalment of fifty dollars and twenty cents. Then the company had come along and taken it away.

'Yeah, times are hard, all right,' he said as we all squatted down on the floor. 'Poverty's a great leveller though: my neighbours used to be domestic servants and porters, millhands and stockyard workers, prostitutes and hoodlums, even respectable laundresses and Baptist preachers. But Ma and I will be bidding farewell to them all soon.'

He sounded so sure of his last statement that I guessed he must have struck it lucky and found a job. But no, he had even better prospects.

'I've got money. I invested in this country, in the government. They owe me. Here, take a good look.'

In the weak glow of the kerosene lamp he showed us some papers. Above his name, 'Mr Henry Jones', was the deed title: *BONUS CERTIFICATE*. I scanned the document and read the fine print at the bottom: *Repayment date: 1 January 1945.*

'But that's thirteen years away!' I blurted out.

Too late I bit my tongue. Why dash the man's last hopes?

He wasn't put off. 'Well spotted, little missy,' he said brightly. 'But, you see, we need the money now. The government's *got* to dish it out right away. It's *our* money; they're just holding it for us. Anyway, it's as good as promised. The bill to pay off the bonus has already passed Congress. It just needs the seal of approval from the Senate. I've been following it all in the papers.'

I smiled, happy for him. It was the first piece of good news I'd heard in a long while. With his bonus money he was planning to move to another town, make a fresh start, maybe dig over a plot of land so that he and his mother could produce their own vegetables, eggs and milk. Here was an American war veteran who still believed in Uncle Sam, in the American way of life.

'Congress will keep its promise to those who risked their lives in the war,' he said with feeling. 'It's got to . . .'

A change suddenly came over Beanpole. The sight of his uncle had somehow depressed him, turned him sour. Perhaps he felt that he'd let me down. Now he saw through the administration's promises, even if Uncle Henry didn't.

'What if Senate doesn't pass the bill?' asked Beanpole in a dull voice.

The grey-haired veteran smiled broadly. 'No way! Congress has given us its word. And that's good enough for me. But . . . just to remind them how desperate we are, a bunch of us are going to Washington. We'll stage a peaceful march around Capitol Hill to show them we're behind the government. Folk are going from all over the country, with their families. Anyways, what with the election due in November, President Hoover wouldn't dare turn us down. He needs our votes.'

'He may need our votes,' snorted Beanpole, 'but he won't lift a finger for the poor. It's all hot air. You're wasting your time, Uncle Henry.'

I felt cross with Beanpole. He was being cruel to his uncle. I was infected by the old man's enthusiasm, even if I didn't share his faith in the system and its empty promises. Still, it would be nice to see the downtrodden get their due for a change. I gave Beanpole a look to say, 'Keep your trap shut!'

'Can we come, too?' I asked.

'It's a free country,' said Uncle Henry with feeling. 'You're welcome. In fact, I've never ridden freight before, so you can show me the ropes, Boxcar Molly. I've no other way of getting there.'

I wondered whether Delaney knew of the Washington march and the hand-out from the government. He was a veteran of the war and might have a few bonus certificates tucked away for a rainy day. So, on parting with Uncle Henry that evening and agreeing to meet two days later, Beanpole and I began the long, cold trek back to East 10th Street.

We found the old soldier sitting on the plank bed darning his socks. 'The Devil finds work for idle hands,' he explained, catching sight of us in the doorway. 'Get out of my light and sit down. It's good to see you two vagrants again. I didn't expect you so soon. I thought you'd be living it up with that pie foreman uncle of yours.'

Beanpole explained all about the rat-infested cellar and his uncle's fate.

'Yep, the poor old blacks have it worse than us poor whites,' Delaney muttered. 'They pay more rent, lose more jobs and get less cash. I'm sorry.'

'There's hope yet, Mr Delaney,' I hastened to reassure him. 'We came to let you know.'

'Oh, yeah,' he growled. 'Let me guess. Hoover's done dropped down dead? Santa Claus is the new President? No? I know, we're going to start a new war to get the nation back to work . . .'

He didn't look up to watch us shake our heads. The old cynic busied himself with his pair of socks.

'Do you have any bonus certificates?' I asked.

'Those worthless scraps of paper,' he snorted.

'Haven't you heard?' I said. 'Congress is going to pay them up early. Beanpole's uncle is going on a march in Washington to celebrate.'

'More fool him,' sighed Delaney. 'I don't believe a word of government promises; nor do I believe in marches. The last one I took part in was back in 1930, a few months after the Crash. Quite a few of us walked to Union Square under a banner that read: *WORK OR WAGES! DON'T STARVE – FIGHT!*

' "You're free to protest," they told us. Shall I tell you what happened?'

He first made us some tea before telling us his story.

'The moment we got to Union Square, the police charged the thirty-five thousand demonstrators with clubs. Women were struck in the face, boys were beaten by gangs of seven or eight policemen, and an old man was knocked down and dragged to his feet, then struck with fist and club. I saw it all with my own eyes.

'And what good did it do? Things only got worse. What we need is a revolution, like they had in Russia. Let those who produce wealth enjoy wealth. Let factory and farm workers run the country.'

Even though Beanpole's uncle had given me a glimmer of hope for change, I leaned towards Delaney's lack of trust of America's leaders. Three long years of travelling round the USA had given me a vivid picture of the hardship and suffering of the people.

Either the government didn't care or it was totally incapable of doing anything about the Depression. If the system had broken down, then it was time to give another one a try.

Up till now Beanpole hadn't shared my distrust of

authority, nor Delaney's hatred of the bosses. Before we'd come to New York, he was like his uncle: his faith in free enterprise was strong enough to believe that someone would come up with a solution.

But now, all of a sudden, his faith seemed knocked out of him.

'They're all the same, these politicians,' Beanpole blurted out. 'They're out to protect the rich and powerful. They couldn't care less about us. What we need is one of our own in the White House – someone to look after the poor.'

We talked on and on, arguing about politics. Although our views differed, Beanpole and I were agreed on one thing: Delaney ought to come with us to Washington. One way or the other, he should be there to cash in on his bonus certificates.

'Well,' he growled, 'if I do strike it rich, I'll eat my hat and buy you vagrants a square meal.'

We settled for that . . . even though he obviously had no hat to eat.

Nine

The Show-down

We spent one cold, hungry night on the streets, and one warm, full-bellied night at the Municipal Lodging. Beanpole and I weren't at all sorry to see the back of New York. On the morning of our planned ride to Washington, in early April 1932, we met up again with Uncle Henry; but there was no sign of Delaney. Maybe he'd decided to paper his walls with the certificates instead.

Down in the railroad yards we were in for a surprise. First, there was a great crowd of people – a couple of hundred at least – looking to ride freight to Washington. And then, a conductor came round wanting to know how many of us there were – 'So I can put on enough boxcars for you guys . . .' He told us that the train staff were with us all the way, even the railroad detectives!

The three of us piled into a boxcar with fifty or sixty others. It was a bit of a squeeze, but we sang and told stories of our experiences of the Depression. By the end of the journey, we felt like we were all part of a big family. Beanpole and I weren't the only non-veterans; a lot of guys had come with their families. One man even had his two grandchildren with him for support.

It felt as if all the travelling we'd been doing finally had a purpose: if only we could get to Washington, things would change. The old soldiers would get their bonus and something would be done to help the poor.

When we arrived, the place seemed crammed with ex-servicemen. Surely the government couldn't refuse all these people?

The first signs weren't good: the city hadn't exactly rolled out the red carpet. It had banned all veterans and their families from the city's flophouses and soup-kitchens. And then we heard that President Hoover had issued a no-nonsense statement: 'NO BONUS!'

He claimed that paying the bonus now would bankrupt the country.

People were furious. They held midnight vigils at the White House and marched around it in shifts all day long.

So there was nowhere to stay for the twenty thousand veterans who'd come from all over America. There were miners from West Virginia, sheet metal workers from Columbus, Georgia, jobless Polish veterans from

Chicago. I met one family – a husband, his wife and their three-year-old boy – who'd spent three months on freight cars coming from California. There was a Mescalero Indian from New Mexico, Chief Running Wolf, all done up in buckskin, head-dress and beads.

Surely the powers-that-be couldn't fail to be moved by such a colourful crowd from every part of the Union. Well, it seemed they could! The day we arrived, by a big majority Senate refused to issue the bonus, on Hoover's advice. Signs went up everywhere: *NO BONUS! GO HOME!*

Some did go home, disheartened and defeated. But most remained: one week, two, three, four. Many had nowhere else to go. Some camped across the Potomac River from the Capitol – a dump known as Anacostia Flats. There the veterans founded a Hooverville, sleeping in lean-tos built out of old newspapers, cardboard boxes, packing crates, bits of tin or tarpaper roofing, every kind of cock-eyed makeshift shelter scraped together from the city dump. These lean-tos were inhabited by families who, whatever their background, all had the same look about them: sunken eyes, hollow cheeks and pale faces.

Anacostia Flats became the veteran army HQ, a ghost camp of a ghost army, with its own medical centre, tactical unit and accommodation office. After reporting to the HQ, newcomers were sent to empty garages and houses, especially the old buildings on Pennsylvania Avenue that were standing vacant. The ghost army just took them over, with no respect for private property.

We were housed in a draughty old garage on the main highway. It had no lighting or heating, but it was dry and suited us as a temporary home. At first, Uncle Henry couldn't believe Hoover's stand. For a few days he sat on a box in the corner of the garage, head in hands. Sometimes his shoulders shook with uncontrollable sobbing. Mostly he just sat there, staring into space. Beanpole and I did our best to cheer him up. But he kept repeating, over and over, 'Was this what we fought for?'

Neither of us were greatly surprised at the turn of events. But now we were here, we were determined that we wouldn't return home with our tails between our legs.

'We're staying put till we get our bonus!' That was the mood.

Neither side would budge. The big question for Hoover now was: how to run the veterans out of town? Four or five times he ordered them out. They ignored him. So he ordered the police chief to drive them out. But *he* refused. Next he ordered the marine commander to chase them out. But *he* refused, too.

Finally the President found someone to shift the bonus marchers: the 'great' all-American hero, General Douglas MacArthur, aided by his right-hand man, Major Dwight Eisenhower.

I'll never forget that day.

MacArthur came down Pennsylvania Avenue on (would you believe it?) a white horse. Behind him were four troops of cavalry, a mounted machine-gun squadron, six whippet tanks, the 12th Infantry in full battledress, three hundred policemen − as well as a squadron of Special Servicemen and Treasury agents. Each infantryman had a gas mask and belt full of tear-gas bombs.

All to shift a rag-taggle army of hungry men, women and children!

At a command from MacArthur, the infantrymen put on their gas masks and hurled the gas bombs into the buildings. Soon the entire block was full of tear gas. If that wasn't enough, they then set fire to the houses. Thousands of men, women and children came streaming out, choking and blinded by the gas. Anyone who didn't move fast enough was jabbed by bayonets or clubbed with rifle butts.

By nightfall the veterans had moved back across the Potomac River into the Hooverville camp. At first light the next day MacArthur's army was preparing for the final assault – on Anacostia Flats. The 12th Infantry marched across the bridge, bayonets at the ready, smoke billowing up behind them from Pennsylvania Avenue.

Beanpole, Uncle Henry and I sat on the ground with thousands of others, barring the way to the camp. It was so one-sided. Here were middle-aged men, defenceless women and children against tanks, tear gas and bayonets.

As the soldiers came closer I noticed a demonstrator suddenly jump to his feet, waving the American flag. An advancing soldier prodded him with his bayonet, saying, 'Get along there, you Commie bum!'

That was it. I heard a familiar growl like approaching thunder. Who else could it be but . . . Delaney!

'Don't push me, son,' he shouted. 'I fought for this flag. I fought for it in France and I'm gonna fight for it here!'

The soldier hit him with the butt of his rifle. Delaney toppled to the ground.

I pushed my way through the soldiers and protesters, finally making it to our old friend. Blood was flowing from his nose and ears, he was breathing in hoarse gasps, and his eyes were closed. As I held up his head, the big Irishman's eyes flickered open.

'Ah, Molly lass. Sorry I missed you. I *had* to come. You were right: even if we lose, *we have to go down fighting.*'

I screamed at the soldiers, 'Call a doctor. Quick! This man's badly hurt.'

The soldiers were young and scared, new soldiers against old soldiers, sons against fathers. But one of them ran back to fetch help.

Delaney lay still, blood staining his collarless shirt and my bare arms.

'Red by blood and red by nature,' he muttered with an attempt at a smile.

Those were his last words. By the time an army medical officer arrived, he was dead, his broken head cradled in my arms.

They didn't tell us how many died that day. Officially, we learned later that Delaney was one of two veterans killed, along with an eleven-week-old baby; two policemen had fractured skulls, many protestors had broken limbs and bayonet cuts, and thousands were injured by gas, some badly.

But the army 'won' the day. Soon all the protestors were driven into the Maryland Woods, and the siege was over. Of course, the President claimed that anarchy had been 'averted'. He had supposedly stopped 'communists from seizing power'. Thanks to the courage and decisiveness of the President, the country had been saved from revolution.

But some brave newsmen told the truth. Paul

Anderson in *The Nation* wrote: *Tanks, gas, sabers, bayonets and fire had been used against unarmed men, women and children to show that the danger of 'insurrection' was real and that the Administration had prepared to meet it.*

It was a shameful day for America . . .

Ten

Remembering the Past

'. . . But it was not a shameful day for *all* Americans. Beanpole and I were proud we'd made a stand. If anyone ever asked us which side we were on, Beanpole and I could surely say we were on the side of America's poor and helpless. We were proud we'd made a stand.' Aunt Molly sat back with her eyes closed, her story told.

Danny and Alice stared at the old woman, rocking to and fro in her creaky chair. It was as if she'd taken them on an amazing journey through America and its past.

But something had been left unsaid.

'Hold on a minute,' said Danny. 'If you're Boxcar Molly, then Uncle Ben must have been . . .'

Aunt Molly opened her eyes and smiled.

'That's right, Danny. Beanpole and I, well, we came through a lot together, good times and bad. But we made it. And there was one thing the hard times could never destroy: the love we had for each other. We got married and lived to see better days.'

'But what happened to Uncle Henry?' asked Alice.

Aunt Molly sighed. 'Once a year old Beanpole and I used to lay flowers on Delaney's grave. Sadly, it wasn't long before we shared the flowers in the same New York veterans' cemetery with Uncle Henry. The Depression finally broke his heart. The white 'red' was buried next to the black 'red, white and blue'. That's America, I guess.'

Alice took a cookie from a plate on the table. 'I'm glad I never had to go without food,' she said.

'Or risk getting shot!' added Danny with a shiver.

'Well,' said Aunt Molly, picking up her knitting, 'thankfully those days are long gone.'

She gazed fondly at Danny and Alice over her glasses. 'You know what, children?' she murmured. 'Before Beanpole passed on, we'd often look back together. They were terrible times. They were remarkable times. Thank goodness you youngsters never had to live through them. All the same, they're part of our history: our shame and our pride. Every person should know about them. It's a story worth telling, isn't it?'

Historical Notes

As the world's most powerful nation, the USA was bound to spread its Depression to other countries. According to the old saying, 'When General Motors sneezes, the rest of the world catches a cold'. The US stock market crash had a domino effect on the Western world: when it crashed, it knocked the others over.

In Europe, Britain and France were badly affected. The impact on Germany, still struggling to recover from defeat in World War I, indirectly led to the Nazis coming to power in 1933.

But it was in America that the slump went deepest.

At the height of the Depression in late 1932 the American people voted President Hoover out, replacing him with the Democrat Franklin Delano Roosevelt. President Roosevelt took office on 4 March 1933 and immediately launched a programme of reform which became known as the 'New Deal'. Slowly the economy began to improve.

The Depression didn't end there, however. It continued all through the 1930s. Towards the end of the decade, things were sliding back again and Americans were becoming disillusioned. Ironically, it was the outbreak of World War II that brought the Depression to an end – by getting people back to work: making bombs, tanks, shells. One nightmare ended as another began.

Further Information

If you would like to find out more about the Great Depression, these books will help:

David Downing, *Twentieth-century Perspectives* (Heinemann Library, 2001)

Stewart Ross, *The Great Depression* (Evans Brothers, 1997)

There are also many websites about the Depression on the Internet. A few are listed below:

www.history1900s.about.com/cs/greatdepression/
This is a timeline of major events surrounding America's Great Depression.

www.library.csi.cuny.edu/dept/history/lavender/
cherries.html
This website has several songs from the Great Depression.

www.senior-center.com/depress.htm

Try this website for recipes and stories from the Great
Depression.

Glossary

Boxcar An enclosed railroad goods wagon.

Bum Another word for a tramp. It also means to beg.

Capitol Hill The seat of US Congress in Washington.

Chain gang A team of convicts chained together and forced to work in the open air.

City stockade A city jail.

Congress The US parliament, consisting of two houses: the upper house or Senate and the House of Representatives.

Dime US currency. There are five cents in a nickel, ten cents in a dime and ten dimes in a dollar.

Dough A slang word for money.

Flophouse A cheap lodging house for vagrants.

Freight A goods train.

Governor Head of a US state.

Great War Another term for the First World War, 1914–1918.

Hobo This is another word for a tramp.

Hooverville A shanty town built by unemployed and destitute people during the Depression. They were named after the President at the time, Herbert C. Hoover.

Jungle A squatters' camp.

Ku Klux Klan An extremist secret society of white people devoted to stopping blacks from getting equality with whites. Members of the Klan disguised themselves in white robes and hoods in order to carry out acts of terrorism and intimidation against black people and their supporters.

Lynch To hang someone.

Panhandle A slang word referring to begging.

Peddle To sell goods, usually in very small quantities.

Skid Row A part of town inhabited by vagrants.

Slammer A slang word for jail.

Soup-kitchen A place dispensing soup to the poor.

Squatter A person who takes possession of empty premises, without the owner's permission.

Vagrant A person without a home or work.

THE STAR HOUSES

Stewart Ross

Snipping away the stitching that held on my yellow star, my mother said defiantly, 'Right! That's simple. From now on we won't wear these silly badges. None of us!' When she had finished, she exclaimed, 'There! Now you're just an ordinary Hungarian like everyone else.' If only it had been that simple.

Bandi Guttmann is a fourteen-year-old Hungarian Jew, living in Budapest in 1944. German forces have occupied the city and life for Bandi and his family is about to become unbearable. Set apart from the rest of the Hungarian community, and denied basic human rights, the family's only weapon is their determination to survive. But in the face of mindless hatred, will the Guttmanns' strength, love and courage be enough to hold them together?

The Star Houses is based on the memoirs of Andor Guttmann.

Another Survivors title from Hodder Wayland

THE WATER PUPPETS

Clive Gifford

Seven white crosses . . . Seven men dead. Xuan shuddered at the thought. What was the point of such death? Seven soldiers must have died right here on this deserted, lonely road. 'Why?' Xuan wondered to himself.

The farmers of Noy Thien village have enough of a war on their hands with the seasons, the monsoon and the soil – they have no reason to fight anything else. But this is Vietnam and it's 1967. The country is divided and American troops have moved in. For thirteen-year-old Xuan and his family, their world is about to be turned upside down. Neighbours are fighting each other and no one is certain who the real enemy is. Can life for Xuan's family ever be the same again?

Another Survivors title from Hodder Wayland

THE ENEMY

James Riordan

It was so pitiful to see. Now and then we'd hear the screaming Stukas diving on these poor, defenceless souls, like eagles on their prey. The sky would be black with them. And they'd send the refugees diving into ditches or under wagons. Why, oh, why did they have to gun down old men, women and children?

War brings out the worst in some people, and the best in others. It's spring 1940 in occupied France when Marie and her mother find themselves looking after two injured soldiers. But one is English and the other is German, and they are sworn enemies. The two patients must not find out about each other. Will the compassion and understanding of one girl and her mother be enough to keep the peace?

ORDER FORM

Other titles in the SURVIVORS series:

0 7502 3311 7 THE STAR HOUSES: A Story from the Holocaust *Stewart Ross*	£9.99	❑
0 7502 3528 4 THE WATER PUPPETS: A Story from Vietnam *Clive Gifford*	£9.99	❑
0 7502 3442 3 THE ENEMY: A Story from World War II *James Riordan*	£9.99	❑
0 7502 3630 2 BROKEN LIVES: A Victorian Mine Disaster *Neil Tonge*	£9.99	❑

All Hodder Children's books are available at your local bookshop or newsagent, or can be ordered direct from the publisher. Just tick the titles you want and fill in the form below. Prices and availability subject to change without notice.

Hodder Wayland, Cash Sales Department, Bookpoint, 130 Milton Park, Abingdon, OXON, OX14 4TD, UK. If you have a credit card, our call team would be delighted to take your order by telephone. Our direct line is *01235 400414* (lines open 9.00 am–6.00 pm Monday to Saturday, 24 hour message answering service). Alternatively you can send a fax on *01235 400454*.

Or please enclose a cheque or postal order made payable to Bookpoint Ltd to the value of the cover price and allow the following for postage and packing: UK & BFPO – £1.00 for the first book, 50p for the second book, and 30p for each additional book ordered up to a maximum charge of £3.00. OVERSEAS & EIRE – £2.00 for the first book, £1.00 for the second book, and 50p for each additional book.

Name ....

Address ....

....

....

If you would prefer to pay by credit card, please complete:
Please debit my Visa/Access/Diner's Card/American Express (delete as applicable) card no:

Signature ....

Expiry Date ....